Cover: Under Golden Gate Bridge

And while the wind began to sweep
  A music out of sheet and shroud,
   We steered her toward a crimson cloud
That landlike slept along the deep.

Alfred, Lord Tennyson

WORLD POINT \ WORLD LINE

Kathleen M. Podolsky

Library of Congress Cataloging in Publications Data

Podolsky, Kathleen M.
  World Point/World Line

1. Photography, Artistic   2. Podolsky, Kathleen M.
 I. Title

TR654.P6   779′.092′4   82-15164
                                      AACR2

ISBN 0-942714-00-8

Graphics: Charlene Carpentier, Ingrid Worthge
Typesetting: ARType, Redwood City, CA 94061
Duotones and Printing: House of Printing, Mt. View, CA 94043

CONTENTS

INTRODUCTION

Poetry and the Visual Arts

One of the clichés of ancient criticism says that every art form yearns to fulfill itself by achieving the condition of some other art form. Architecture strives to be like sculpture, dance like music, and poetry like painting. The relationship between the pairs is not only one of simple ambition; the one is really a kind of diminished version of the other, and in fact would be the other if it could be brought to its perfection. Thus the second member of the pair provides the principal analogy for understanding the first. If you want to know what poetry is like, all you have to do is turn to Horace, who got it from Simonides, and he'll tell you straight enough: *"ut pictura poesis,"* it's like a painting.

From the very beginning there have been poems which have tried to function as some sort of visual record, a kind of verbal snapshot, of a particular object. Offhand one thinks of Homer's description of the shield of Achilles, "The Dream of the Rood," Coleridge's "Kubla Khan," Tennyson's "The Eagle," Shelley's "Ozymandias," and almost anything by Crashaw. In the Seventeenth Century there was a whole tradition of satire called the "Advice to the Painter" poems; in our own century, there was an international movement in poetry called "Imagism".

If you wanted a thumbnail definition of poetry—"Poetry" in the old sense—it would be the concrete use of language. Unlike the laboratory report or newspaper that is abstract and full of general terms, poetry makes us see things. The distinguishing mark of poetry is the image—the metaphor, the simile. It is the visual quality of poetry that makes us think of it as less a medium of expression than a kind of window onto reality, an avenue to the truth of experience more direct and immediate than science. That is why the poet is often seen as a prophet.

We have all heard the old saying that "a picture is worth a thousand words." This is in fact true—provided that those thousand words aren't poetry. Compare a story in say, "Newsweek" with the pictures which illustrate it. Those of us who are old enough, read about the war in Vietnam until our minds were numb, but who can ever forget the photograph of the little girl running naked down a road with her back covered with flaming napalm? One of the reasons that particular conflict was so unpopular was that we had to witness it, visually, every night on the Seven O'Clock News.

Poetry and painting—or photography—works its magic by presenting us with a stripped-down, focused version of reality, something from which all the extraneous material has been removed so that it compels our attention. As Aristotle pointed out, a line drawing of, say, a horse will show us much more strikingly what horses are like than hours of watching the real animal. We point to the drawing and say, "yes, that's it. That's what it's like."

A poem or a photograph doesn't impress us so much *because* it is nearer the truth of everyday experience—how could it be that?—as because it is somehow subtly at variance with that truth. This sounds like a paradox—art conveys the sense of reality by differing from reality. It is a paradox, but it is no less true for being so.

F. Scott Fitzgerald once wrote that, "life is much more successfully looked at from a single window, after all." In other words, sometimes we can most advantageously see the whole by concentrating on the part. The part is all we ever really get anyway—there is no certainty in our knowledge of the universe, only approximations—so perhaps, then, art doesn't do so badly, after all.

In order to understand what I'm driving at, look at any of the photographs or any stanza of poetry in this book. Ask yourself, what makes it attractive, or pleasing, or interesting? The answer, of course, is not that it is so like what it portrays or describes, but rather precisely the opposite. It is its subtle strangeness that gives it its appeal, and this, again, is equally true of both poetry and the visual arts. The photograph is different from its subject—no rose ever really looked like that—and yet when was the last time you ever looked at a real rose as closely as you are looking at this one?

Critics of poetry have long since dismissed the idea that it really is, as Horace claimed, "like a picture." The analogy is false; language works in an entirely different way. But does it? Possibly no one can answer that question for anyone else. The pictures and the poetry are here before you, so you'll have the pleasure of deciding this question for yourself.

Nicholas Guild

FORWARD

The term *World Point* was devised by the mathematician Minkowski and Albert Einstein to denote an event occurring in three dimensional space at a certain time; *World Line* applies to a similar but non-stationary occurrence. These bold concepts gave our universe its 'fourth dimension' and helped to explain why observers might see the same event differently as a result of variations in time, location, or perspective. Insofar as fine art photography stretches and contracts temporal events and strives to project images out and away from the two dimensional flat page it too creates new dimensions. That is why *World Point* and *World Line* naturally adapted themselves to the title.

In this age of advanced technology, where both color photography and color printing have attained such high degrees of fidelity, the decision to stay with the pure "silver image" demands an explanation. As a vehicle for understanding you are asked to consider music where we enjoy both grandiloquent orchestrations as well as solo presentations. To me the black and white print is the equivalent of solo work. It epitomizes the highest form of virtuosity because it has to stand on its own merits and has no elaborate orchestrations to bolster its weaknesses or hide its faults. Perhaps, after reading the *haiku* poetry you might gain a better feeling for the black and white print—because both art forms have been refined down to their quintessences.

John Stuart Mill stated "the word 'poetry' imports something quite peculiar in its nature; . . . something which does not even require the instrument of words, but can speak through . . . musical sounds, and even through the visable ones which are the language of sculpture, painting and architecture . . ." Had photography been known at that time, Mill would certainly have included it in his commentary.

Taking license from John Stuart Mill, I placed my photographs within the context of words—*haiku* and conventional poetry—and the total effect grew to be greater than the sum of its parts. Images evoked by verse superimposed themselves upon the print, and conversely, the photographs delineated a segment of the poets meaning. This juxtaposition of objective viewing with subjective interpretations creates an additional dimension. Try it; keep the pictures in mind as you assimilate the words. Or as T. S. Eliot said:

> "Oh, do not ask, "What is it?"
> Let us go and make our visit."

February 1982
Belmont, California

Kathleen M. Podolsky

. . . It is not now as it hath been of yore;—
Turn wheresoe'er I may,
By night or day,
The things which I have seen I now can see no more.

William Wordsworth

Patriarch
Kweilin, China

That time of year thou mayst in me behold
When yellow leaves, or none, or few, do hang
Upon those boughs which shake against the cold,
Bare ruin'd choirs, where late the sweet birds sang.

William Shakespeare

Sycamore Leaves

The mansion from its firm foundation
Up to its roof was past all praise,
Expressing the discrimination,
The noble taste of bygone days.

Alexander Pushkin

Yusupov Palace
Archangel, U.S.S.R.

Add a pair of wings
To a pepper-pod, you would
Make a dragon-fly.

Bashō

Dragonfly

. . . Yet shall some tribute of regret be paid
When her long life hath reached its final day:
Men are we, and must grieve when even the Shade
Of that which once was great is passed away.

William Wordsworth

House
Maine Woods

Work without Hope draws nectar in a sieve,
And Hope without an object cannot live . . .

Samuel Taylor Coleridge

Children of Sein Bight
Belize, Central America

. . . And is not time even as love is, undivided and
paceless?

But if in your thought you must measure time into
seasons, let each season encircle all the other seasons,

And let today embrace the past with remembrance and
the future with longing.

Kahil Gibran

Glass and Sand Construction by Julianne Frizzel

Drifting clouds, on high
And below, pass each other
In the autumn sky.

Bonchō

Ranch Scene
Sierra Nevada Mountains, Nevada

. . . In spite of all that beauty may disown
In your harsh features, Nature doth embrace
Her lawful offspring in Man's art; and Time,
Pleased with your triumphs o'er his brother Space,
Accepts from your bold hands the proffered crown
Of hope, and smiles on you with cheer sublime.

William Wordsworth

Croatian Church
Jackson, California

Long the summer day . . .
Patterns on the ocean sand . . .
Our idle footprints

Shiki

Beach
Point Reyes , California

Cat! who hast pass'd thy grand climacteric,
How many mice and rats hast in thy days
Destroy'd? — How many tit bits stolen? Gaze
With those bright languid segments green, and prick
Those velvet ears—but pr'ythee do not stick
Thy latent talons in me—and upraise
Thy gentle mew—and tell me all thy frays
Of fish and mice, and rats and tender chick.

John Keats

A cat called Poon

. . . Ordain'd to move when others please,
Not for my own content or ease;
But toss'd and buffetted about,
Now in the water and now out . . .

William Cowper

Sea Washed Seeds
Belize, Central America

. . . Hour by hour the caisons reach down to the rock of the earth
        and hold the building to a turning planet.
Hour by hour the girders play as ribs and reach out and hold
        together the stone walls and floors.
Hour by hour the hand of the mason and the stuff of the mortar clinch
        the pieces and parts to the shape an architect voted.
Hour by hour the sun and the rain, the air and the rust, and the press
        of time running into centuries, play on the building
        inside and out and use it . . .

Carl Sandburg

Prentice Hospital
Chicago, Illinois

See how the orient dew,
Shed from the bosom of the morn
Into the blowing roses,
Yet careless of its mansion new,
For the clear region where 'twas born,
Round in its self incloses;
And in its little globe's extent,
Frames as it can its native element . . .

Andrew Marvell

Golden Wave Roses

There is a solitude of space
A solitude of sea
A solitude of death, but these
Society shall be
Compared with that profounder site
That polar privacy
A soul admitted to itself—
Finite Infinity.

Emily Dickinson

Birch Forest
Ukraine, U.S.S.R.

Now let no charitable hope
Confuse my mind with images
Of eagle and of antelope;
I am in nature none of these.

I was, being human, born alone;
I am, being woman, hard beset;
I live by squeezing from a stone
The little nourishment I get.

In masks outrageous and austere
The years go by in single file;
But none has merited my fear,
And none has quite escaped my smile.

                         Elinor Wylie

Auntie
Annetta Siegfried

There's music along the river
          For Love wanders there,
Pale flowers on his mantle,
          Dark leaves on his hair.

                    James Joyce

Oxford Canal
Fenny Compton, England

. . . A door that will not open, sick and numb,
I listen for a word that will not come,
And know, at last, I may not enter more . . .

Hermann Hagedorn

Back Door
Pittville Store, California

The trees are in their autumn beauty,
The woodland paths are dry,
Under the October twilight the water
Mirrors a still sky; . . .

W. B. Yeats

Tarn
Inverness Shire, Scotland

Beside the unwashed window the spring day
Passed unemployed. Behind the wall I heard
A voice singing, my wife's, as restlessly
Rehearsing tedium as a caged bird.

Alexander Blok

Farm House
Carson City, Nevada

. . . On their own feet they came, or on shipboard,
Camel-back, horse-back, ass-back, mule-back
Old civilizations put to the sword.
Then they and their wisdom went to rack: . . .*

W. B. Yeats

*(Yeats to Dorothy Wellesley, July 6, 1935).

". . . someone has sent me a present of a great piece
(of lapis lazuli) carved by some Chinese sculptor . . .
Ascetic, pupil, hard stone, eternal theme of the sensual
east. The heroic cry in the midst of despair. But no,
I am wrong, the east has its solutions always and there-
fore knows nothing of tragedy. It is we, not the east,
that must raise the heroic cry."

Festival Crowd
Taiyuan, China

. . . Thou, silent form, dost tease us out of thought
As doth eternity: . . .

John Keats

Bahā'ī House of Worship
Wilmette, Illinois

The Worldly Hope men set their Hearts upon
Turns Ashes—or it prospers: and anon,
Like Snow upon the Desert's dusty Face,
Lighting a little hour or two—is gone.

Ruba'iyat

Kennedy Mine
Jackson, California

When the flush of a new born sun fell first on Eden's green
        and gold,
Our father Adam sat under the Tree and scratched with a stick
        in the mold;
And the first rude sketch that the world had seen was joy
        to his mighty heart,
Till the Devil whispered behind the leaves:
        "It's pretty, but is it Art?"

                              Rudyard Kipling

Balustrade
Victorian Mansion

Ha! ha! the caverns of my hollow mountains,
My cloven fire-crags, sound-exulting fountains
Laugh with a vast and inextinguishable laughter . . .

Percy Bysshe Shelley

Thunder Mountain
Yellowstone National Park, Wyoming

. . . O'er come by labor, and bowed down by time,
Feel you the barren flattery of a rhyme?
Can poets soothe you, when you pien for bread,
By winding myrtle round your ruined shed?

George Crabbe

Antigua
Guatamala

. . . And winter slumbering in the open air
Wears on his smiling face a dream of Spring!

Samuel Taylor Coleridge

Winter Scene
Fresno County, California

Who made the world and ruleth it, He hangeth on a stalk,
For I am in His image made, and all this tinkling tide
Is but a sliding drop of rain between His petals wide.

                              W. B. Yeats

Rain Drop

. . . One adequate support
For the calamities of mortal life
Exists, one only;—an assured belief
That the procession of our fate, howe'er
Sad or disturbed, is ordered by a Being
Of infinite benevolence and power;
Whose everlasting purposes embrace
All accidents, converting them to good.

William Wordsworth

Feed Store
Fall River Mills, California

ACKNOWLEDGEMENTS

From "Skyscraper" in CHICAGO POEMS by Carl Sandburg, copyright 1916 by Holt, Rinehart and Winston, Inc., copyright 1944 by Carl Sandburg. Reprinted by permission of Harcourt Brace Jovanovich, Inc.

From "The Indian God" from COLLECTED POEMS of William Butler Yeats (New York; Macmillan, 1956)

From "The Swans at Coole" from COLLECTED POEMS of William Butler Yeats, copyright 1919 by Macmillan Publishing Co., Inc., renewed 1947 by Bertha Georgie Yeats.

Two Haiku from A PEPPER-POD, Classic Japanese Poems Together with Original Haiku by Shoson, by Bashō and Bonchō, copyright 1956 by Kenneth Yasuda.

From LOTUS BLOSSOMS Haiku by Shiki, translated by Peter Beilenson, copyright 1970 by The Peter Pauper Press, Inc.

From COLLECTED POEMS of Elinor Wylie, "Let No Charitable Hope," copyright 1932 by Alfred A. Knopf, Inc., Authorized Publisher.

From THE NORTON ANTHOLOGY OF ENGLISH LITERATURE, Volume 2, from "Steamboats, Viaducts, and Railways" by William Wordsworth and from "Lapis Lazuli" by William Butler Yeats, copyright 1962 by W. W. Norton and Company, Inc.

Sculpture titled "Stairways to Heaven", construction completed summer of 1981 by Julianne Frizzell.